BOOK OF

VA**C**ATION PLANNING

HOME PURCHASE

HOBBI**E**S

HALLOWEEN **C**OSTUMES

KITCHEN UTENSILS

TAI**L**GATE PARTY

G **I** FTS FOR HER

RE**S**TAURANT CHOICES

OP**T**IONS FOR A NIGHT OUT

GARAGE **S** ALE PREPARATIONS

AND CHOICES

The Complete Guide to Daily Decision Making

By

Patrick Shearer

ISBN: 1-4033-7996-3 (e-book)
ISBN: 1-4033-7997-1 (Paperback)

Library of Congress Control Number: 2002094741

This book is printed on acid free paper.

Printed in the United States of America
Bloomington, IN

1stBooks — rev. 11/01/02

INTRODUCTION

Have you ever had company come into town but can't think of a thing to do to keep them entertained? Do you have a week off this summer but can't figure out where to go? Are you considering purchasing a home but don't have the foggiest idea how to get started? If the answer to any of these questions is, "yes", then The Book of Checklists and Choices is for you. The book is loaded with dozens of simple checklists designed to guide you through situations like these. You'll be able to use the checklists to plan the perfect party, purchase the perfect gift and pick the perfect vacation destination. To top it all off this book will save you time, money and loads of aggravation.

HOW TO USE THIS BOOK

Browse through the check list index. When you have to plan an event or make a decision simply find the checklist that applies to your situation. There are usually a few blank lines at the end of each list to add items specific to your event. If your situation is not in the book you can use the blank sheets at the back to build your own customized checklist. Actually, it was a crumpled collection of hand written lists that formed the foundation for this book. We trust you will find the collection as helpful as we have.

INDEX

PARTY PLANNING

GENERIC PARTY PREPARATIONS

✔ ☐	ACTION	NOTES
	PREPARATIONS	
	Pick a theme	
	Pick the day	
	Pick the time	
	How much can you afford to spend?	
	Complete the guest list	
	Create a map with directions	
	Purchase invitations	
	Fill out and mail invitations—note if RSVP is required	
	Volunteers to bring extra chairs and tables	
	Volunteers to help with set-up	
	Select the food and format (e.g. pot luck?)	
	DECISIONS AND PURCHASES	
	Beverages: Liquor, beer, wine, soda, water	
	Paper Products: Cups, plates, utensils	
	Trash cans and trash bags for clean-up	
	Ice	
	Ashtrays	
	Condiments: Mustard, ketchup, mayonnaise	
	Cake and candles	
	PARTY SPECIFICS	
	Layout: where to put the food & beverages?	
	Music and entertainment	
	Games: board games, cards	
	Where to hang the coats and put the shoes	
	Extra televisions (for sporting events)	

TAILGATE PARTY PREPARATIONS

✔ ☐	THINGS TO BRING	NOTES
	Coolers	
	Table	
	Chairs	
	Tablecloth	
	Food	
	* Meats, cheese, snacks, vegetables	
	Utensils to serve the food	
	Beverages	
	* Soda, beer, wine, water	
	Liquor, mixers, olives	
	Coffee or hot chocolate	
	Cups, glasses, knives, spoons, forks	
	Ice	
	Toothpicks	
	Football	
	Napkins	
	Plastic garbage bags	
	Portable TV or radio	
	Tickets	
	Camera	
	Blankets	
	Tobacco products	
	Sign or marker so people can find you	
	Sunglasses	

Patrick Shearer

PARTY FOOD AND BEVERAGES

SNACKS
Potato Chips

Pretzels

Vegetable Tray with Dip

Cheese Curls

Nuts

Cheese ball

Crackers

APPETIZERS
Chicken Wings

Small Sausages

Meat Tray

MAIN COURSE
Chicken

Ribs

Hamburgers

Lasagna

Hot Dogs

Steak

Bratwurst

Shish ka-bobs

Polish Sausage

BEVERAGES
Soda (Diet & regular)

Beer (Regular & Light)

Wine

Wine Coolers

Liquor

Fruit Juice

Bottled Water

Club Soda

Coffee

Hot Chocolate

VEGETABLES
Potato

Carrots

Mixed Vegetables

Salad

Potato salad

Macaroni salad

Broccoli

Cauliflower

DESSERTS
Cake

Pie

Ice Cream

Cream Puffs

Doughnuts

Fruit

CONDIMENTS
Ketchup

Mustard

Steak Sauce

Barbeque Sauce

Cheese slices

Mayonnaise

Pickles

Salad dressing

HALLOWEEN COSTUMES

Vampire	Witch	Knight in armor
Frankenstein	Pumpkin	Damsel in distress
Werewolf	Police officer	Canadian Mountie
Dracula	Fireman	Joan of Arc
Romeo or Juliet	Hobo	Pope
President	Judge	Chicken and Egg
First Lady	Lawyer	Mailman
Priest or monk	Cat	Chef
Nurse	Dog	Raggedy Ann or Andy
Doctor	Soldier	Sailor
Piece of candy	Rock & roll star	Waiter or waitress
Moon	Astronaut	Mobster
Sun	Cigarette or cigar	Gambler
Clown	Santa or Mrs. Claus	Easter bunny
Man (if woman)	Easter bunny	Skeleton
Woman (if man)	Historical figure	Action hero
Ballerina	Computer	Radio
Movie star	TV star	TV set
French maid	Butler	Tree or shrub
Race car driver	Mechanic	Ghost

Patrick Shearer

SIGNIFICANT OTHER

Patrick Shearer

GIFTS FOR SIGNIFICANT OTHER

Perfume, lotion, cologne	Power tools	Nice shirt
Magazine subscription	Gift certificate	Football
Lawn mower	Tennis racket	Driving range membership
Golf clubs	Health club membership	Water skis
Golf balls	Manicure	New furnace or A/C
Book	Pedicure	Car detailed
Basketball	Season tickets to???	Fishing rod or equipment
Professional massage	Home improvement coupon	Hunting gear
No ties or socks	Camcorder	Painting, prints, pictures
Beer of the month club	Cable or satellite TV	Let them sleep in
Cigar of the month club	Auto racing tickets	Bat and mitt
CD/Cassettes	No chores for a night	Bicycle
DVD or VCR	Items for hobby	Roller Blades
Television	Foot rub	Party
Night out with friends	Wash their car	Chips for a casino
Getaway weekend	Cellular phone	Coat or jacket
Sunday brunch	Golf or tennis lessons	On line membership
New car	Snow skis and equipment	Jet ski
Breakfast in bed	Country club membership	Skateboard
Vacation	Vinyl siding	Calculator
Bottle of liquor	Paint the house	Jewelry
Time share condominium	Poker table	Kitchen utensil or appliances
New roof	Cigars	Balloon ride
Lingerie	Plane tickets	Lottery tickets
Limousine for a night	Chain saw	Fax machine
Computer	Meal of their choice	Home copy machine
Hand tools	Snowmobile	Lawn tractor
Board games	New printer	Home exercise equipment
New carpet	Motorcycle	Caribbean cruise
Watch the kids	Sky write "Happy B-Day"	Flowers at work
Take the day off	Let them choose the gift	Art object
Put the photos in an album	Make a video of photographs	Create their biography

Use the blank columns to add your own items to keep track of past gifts

PLANNING A NIGHT OUT

Opera
Movies
Stage Play
Dinner out
Dinner theatre
Dinner train
Star gazing
Boat ride
Long walk
Concert
Comedy club
Carnival
Church festival
Coffee house
Bowling
Miniature golfing
Roller skating
Karaoke
Bookstore
Professional sporting event
College sporting event
Nightclub for dancing
Nightclub with live music
Cigar bar
Double date
Church bingo
Casino
Library
Walk to your favorite restaurant
Get a hotel for a night
Visit an art gallery or show
Drive to a waterside restaurant
Cards or a board game with friends
Rent a limousine

CHOOSING A RESTAURANT

BIG PICTURE
Dressy or casual?
Dine in, carryout or delivery
Cost
How much time do we have
How far do we want to travel
Sit down, buffet or cafeteria style

FOOD TYPES
Beef
Chicken
Pasta
Asian
Vegetarian
Fish
Pizza
Sandwiches

NATIONALITIES
French
Thai
Vietnamese
Italian
Greek
Chinese
Mid-eastern
Mexican
American

WAYS TO PAMPER YOURSELF (OR SOMEONE ELSE)

Take a nap

Rent a video

Get a manicure

Get a pedicure

Listen to music

Be a couch potato

Go to the gym

Eat your favorite food

Read a book

Read the newspaper

Read a magazine

Get a massage

Get a tan

Take a warm bath

Take a long shower

Buy yourself a present

Hide your "to do" list

Call an old friend

Get a hug

Give a hug

Meditate

Tell someone you love them

Take a walk in the woods

Go on a retreat

Go golfing

Watch a ball game

Play with your pet

Read a joke book

Take some keep breaths

Work on your hobby

Do some yard work

Plan a vacation

Play laser tag or paint ball

Go boating

Surf the web

Play solitaire

Crossword puzzle

Clean the house

Roll coins

Collect something

Read greeting cards

Put photos in an album

Paint or draw a picture

Call a new friend

Patrick Shearer

BABIES AND CHILDREN

FIRST BABY PREPARATIONS

✔ ☐	ACTION	NOTES
	EARLY PREPARATIONS	
	Save some money	
	Day care preparations (if required)	
	Select a pediatrician-ask around	
	Take a baby class	
	Buy a good reference book	
	Develop a short list of names	
	Baby shower	
	Select a room for the baby	
	Take to some veterans for tips	
	INITIAL PURCHASES	
	Baby cleaning suppliers (soap, towel, wash cloth)	
	Baby medical supplies	
	Wipes	
	Bottles and nipples	
	Bouncie or swing	
	Breast milk pump	
	Camcorder	
	Camera	
	Car seat	
	Changing table	
	Cloth diapers for burp cloths	
	Crib and mattress	
	Crib sheets and pads	
	Disposable diapers	
	Lots of one piece outfits	
	Stroller	
	Tub for baths	
	Crib bumper pad	
	THINGS THAT CAN WAIT A FEW MONTHS	
	High chair	
	Child proofing devices	
	Baby gates	
	Toys	
	Stuffed animals	

Patrick Shearer

GIRL NAMES

Ainsley
Ann
Autumn
Betty
Brianna
Carman
Carrie
Cathy
Cherri
Cheryl
Christina
Claire
Connie
Debbie
Delores
Doris
Dorothy
Elizabeth
Eve
Felicity
Francis
Gail
Hanna
Helen
Ingrid
Isabelle

Katherine
Katie
Kristin
Laura
Lavonne
Linda
Lisa
Lois
Loretta
Lori
Lorraine
Lucy
Madeline
Margaret
Mary
Nicole
Paula
Phyllis
Samantha
Sonia
Susan
Tamara
Tammy
Wanda
Wendy

Patrick Shearer

BOY NAMES

Aaron	Jeffrey
Abraham	Jerry
Adam	Joel
Alec	John
Alexander	Jose
Allen	Joseph
Andrew	Keith
Brandon	Kelly
Brant	Kenneth
Brendon	Lawrence
Bret	Mark
Brian	Matthew
Briant	Michael
Bruce	Miles
Burns	Mitchell
Caleb	Nathan
Carter	Nelson
Clifton	Nicholas
Curtis	Norman
Daniel	Patrick
Darryl	Paul
David	Peter
Donald	Phillip
Douglas	Raymond
Earl	Richard
Edward	Robert
Eric	Rocco
Ethan	Ronald
Frank	Samuel
Frasier	Stephen
George	Steven
Gerald	Stuart
Glenn	Sylvester
Gordon	Terry
Gregory	Theodore
Harold	Thomas
Henry	Timothy
Herbert	Todd
Hugh	Ward
Ivan	Wayne
Jack	Wesley
Jacob	William
James	

GIFTS FOR A CHILD

Money	Savings Bond	Airplane ride
Gift certificate	Stock certificate	Television
Action figures	Pony	Radio
Dolls	Pet	Video or DVD
Board games	Hat	CD or cassette
Video games	Shoes	Calculator
Toy store visit	Lottery tickets	Items for their hobby
Sporting event	Books	Sports equipment
Go fishing	Magazine subscription	Bicycle
Clothes	Visit the zoo	Skateboard
Balloon ride	Children's museum	Roller skates
Play or concert	Fun restaurant	Ear piercing
Throw them a party	Go cart	Model kit
Sand box	Basketball hoop	Pool table
Pool	Playhouse	Ping pong table
Blocks	Toy logs	Construction set
Perfume	Wall poster	Painting, picture
Camera and film	Camcorder	Candy
Jewelry	Jet ski	Crayons or markers
Playing cards	Internet access	Coloring book
Educational toys	Personal telephone line	Squirt gun
Collector coins	No chores for a week	Bank account

PACKING FOR A BABY

✔ ☐	ITEM FOR BABY
	Bottles
	Nipples
	Liners
	Bottle plunger
	Formula
	Baby food
	Distilled water
	Baby cereal
	Spoons
	Bibs
	Diapers
	Wipes
	Rash ointment
	Breast pump
	Wash clothes
	Towels
	Baby detergent
	Baby soap
	Burp cloths
	Toys
	Playpen
	Playpen sheets
	Quilt or blanket to crawl on
	Favorite video tapes
	Camera
	Camcorder
	High chair
	Thermometer
	Medicine
	Pacifiers
	Socks
	Shoes
	Tops
	Pants
	One piece outfits
	Coat, hat and gloves
	Favorite foods

BIG EVENTS

PURCHASING A VEHICLE

THINGS TO CONSIDER	NOTES
New or used?	
Purchase or lease?	
Car, truck or sport utility vehicle?	
Convertible or hard top?	
Cost, affordable monthly payment	
Cost for insurance	
Manual or automatic transmission?	
Number of doors	
Audio system	
Length of warranty desired	
Car reputation and reliability record	
Size of engine, vehicle performance	
Trunk space, room to carry items	
Usual and maximum number of passengers	
Bench or bucket seat?	
Cloth seats or leather?	
Safety ratings	
Re-sale potential	
Color	
Fuel economy	
Preferred make or model (manufacturer)	

PURCHASING A HOME

THINGS TO CONSIDER	NOTES
Big Picture	
Location (Outline boundaries on a map)	
Traffic level—court or through street?	
Noise level—airport, rail road, busy street	
Proximity to shopping, groceries, hospital	
Quality of the local school system	
Timetable: When do you want to move in?	
Financial Considerations	
Cost of home (maximum amount to finance)	
Affordable monthly payment	
Complete loan pre-approval to confirm price range	
Select type of loan (duration, fixed, adjustable)	
Home Specifics	
Type of home (colonial, bungalow, ranch)	
Exterior—brick or siding	
Square footage desired	
Number of bedrooms	
Number of bathrooms	
Fireplace required?	
Separate living room and dining room required?	
Consider appliance conveyance—dishwasher, fridge	
Garage: attached or separate? Size?	
Central air conditioning	
Size of lot and lawn	
Getting Ideas	
Attend several open houses	
Select a realtor	
Review home listings	
Check realtor internet sights	
Things to Watch Out For	
Age of the furnace and hot water heater	
Age of the roof and number of layers	
Check for water damage in basement	
Estimate cost for home updates required	
Resale potential	
Tax burden—check if they will increase	
Location of the washer/dryer hook-up	
Neighbors	

GETTING READY TO MOVE

✔ ☐	ACTION	NOTES
	Set the day/dates	
	Move yourself or hire movers?	
	Determine which furniture will be used at the new location	
	Have a garage sale	
	Throw out old stuff	
	Gather boxes	
	Gather paper/bubble wrap for packing	
	Carton tape	
	Mark boxes with room destination	
	Get helpers	
	Notify utility companies to change service	
	Make a list of people/institutions requiring change of address notification	
	Leave vacuum, rags, trash bags and cleaning supplies out to clean old house	
	Radio or music during move	
	Blankets/sheets to cover carpet during the move	
	Food and beverages for helpers	

GARGAGE OR YARD SALE PREPARATIONS

✔ ☐	ACTION	NOTES
	Pick the day and dates	
	Select hours sale will be open	
	Clean out the attic and basement	
	Get city permits (if required)	
	Line up volunteers to help	
	Consider a combined sale with family or friends	
	Tables for merchandise	
	Hangars	
	Clothes racks	
	Price tags	
	Bags and boxes for purchased items	
	Signs for front of house and street corners	
	Newspaper advertisement	
	Cash register or cash drawer	
	Change—coins and currency	
	Chairs for the sellers	
	Consider how low you will go on some prices	
	Back-up plan for storage in case of rain	

SETTING UP AN APARTMENT

✔ ☐	ITEM	NOTES
	KITCHEN	
	Dinner plates, small plates, bowls	
	Silverware	
	Glasses and cups	
	Eating utensils—knife, forks, spoons,	
	Large (serving) utensils	
	Pitcher	
	Can opener, measuring cups, hand mixer	
	Pots and pans	
	Dish towels and wash clothes	
	Plastic wrap, trash bags, aluminum foil	
	Dishwasher soap, sink dish soap, cleaning solutions	
	BATHROOM	
	Cleaners	
	Toiletries (shampoo, razors, toothpaste, toothbrush)	
	Basic medicines (bandages, aspirin, anti-acid)	
	Bars of soap	
	LIVING ROOM	
	Couch	
	Coffee tables	
	Chairs	
	TV	
	Entertainment center	
	Lamps	
	Stereo	
	BEDROOM	
	Bed	
	Desk	
	Nightstands	
	Lamps	
	Dresser	
	Mirror	
	OTHER	
	Laundry soap	
	Flashlight	
	Basic tools (pliers, screwdriver)	
	Light bulbs	
	Extension cords	

WEDDING PLANNING

THINGS TO CONSIDER	NOTES
EARLY DECISIONS	
Time of year (spring, summer, fall)	
Location (inside, outside, church, home)?	
Day of week	
Date	
Time	
Size of wedding, number of guests	
How much can we afford to spend?	
Will we get any financial help?	
Reserve the church or site for wedding	
Reserve the hall for the reception	
Select the wedding party	
Guest list	
Prepare map to ceremony and reception	
Select the invitations	
CEREMONY SPECIFICS	
Wedding gown	
Tuxedoes for groomsman	
Bridesmaid dresses	
Flowers	
Transportation for wedding and reception	
Priest or minister	
Ushers	
Wedding license	
Videographer	
Photographer	
RECEPTION SPECIFICS	
Food and serving style (buffet, sit-down)	
Beverages	
Decorations	
Seating arrangement	
Gifts for wedding party	
OTHER	
Rehearsal dinner planning (day/date, time, location, attendance)	
Activities for the day after the wedding	
Honeymoon plans and timing (consider waiting one week for the honeymoon)	

HONEYMOON IDEAS

Cruises (Caribbean, Alaskan, Mediterranean, South American, Far East, Tahiti, Hawaiian)	Michigan's Upper Peninsula
Rent an RV and travel the U.S.	Golf vacation
All inclusive resort	Any beach
Rent a cottage	Las Vegas
Ski resort	New York
Rent a house boat	Chicago
Far East	Bed and breakfast tour
Latin America	Mexico
Tour Europe	Atlanta
African safari	Low budget hotels
Hawaii	Follow old Route 66
Rent a timeshare	Amusement parks
Tour the U.S. by train	Toronto
Northeast (Maine, Massachusetts)	Canadian Rockies
East Coast (Washington D.C., Virginia)	Backpacking
Southeast (Carolinas)	Mountain climbing
South (Mississippi, Louisiana)	Fly around the world
Southwest (Arizona, Nevada)	Motorcycle tour
Midwest (Illinois, Indiana)	Bicycle tour
North (Dakotas, Wyoming)	Ancestors/family history vacation
Northwest (Oregon, Washington)	
California (San Francisco, Los Angeles)	
Florida (Orlando, St. Augustine, Naples)	

WEDDING GIFT IDEAS

Cash
Item from the gift registry
China setting or piece
Glassware
Flatware
Everyday dinnerware
Serving utensils
Wedding anniversary book
Gift certificate for honeymoon
Gift certificate for restaurant
Art work
Pay for some portion of the wedding (e.g. transportation)
Blessing from the Pope or religious leader
Congratulations from the President (just write the White House)
Frame wedding invitation
Gift certificate for store purchase (e.g. home improvement)
Hotel stay for first honeymoon night
Cable TV for three months
Interior designer consulting visit
Dried flower arrangement
Crystal vase or bowl
Picnic basket
Camcorder
Camera and film
Kitchen appliances
Knife set
Major appliance (e.g. washer and dryer)
Electronic devices
Computer software
Book on being married
Gift certificate for financial consultant

LIFE CHOICES

MY PERFECT PARTNER

CRITERIA	PRIORITY (High/Medium/Low)	WHAT I'M LOOKING FOR
Age		Older, younger, same age?
Personal Traits		Serious, happy
Sense of humor		
Height/Weight/Appearance		
Partner's family background		
Drinker or not?		
Smoker or not?		
Hobbies and interests		
Educational level		
Profession		
Do they have/want children?		
Marital history		Single, divorced
Religious or spiritual life		
Activity Level		Likes to be busy or settled?
Their perfect night out		Similar to mine?
Musical tastes		
Fancy or simple person		
Their vacation preferences		Similar to mine?
Cooking skills		
Sloppy or neat		

Patrick Shearer

CHOOSING A COLLEGE OR UNIVERSITY

QUESTIONS TO ASK?	PRIORITY (High/Medium/Low)	NOTES
Location—how close do I want to be to home?		
Cost—what can I afford?		
Curriculum—what field do I want to study?		
School reputation—is the school recognized in that field?		
Variety—if I change my mind does the school have other specialties?		
Friends—do I know anyone at the school?		
Parents—do they have a strong preference? If so, why?		
Loyalty—is there a school I've always liked?		
Public or private preferred? Religious affiliation desired?		
Sororities or fraternities—does the school have them?		
Employment—does the school have a placement service?		
Experience—does the school offer work study opportunities?		
Have I visited the campus before making my decision?		
Is there anyone who has attended the school that I can speak with?		

Patrick Shearer

GETTING TO KNOW YOURSELF

QUESTIONS TO ASK YOUSELF	EXAMPLES	NOTES
What people do I admire most and why?	Movie star, politician, athlete, scholar, soldier, doctor?	
What values are the most important to me?	Hard work, integrity, perseverance, loyalty	
What do I love to do more than anything else?	Sports, write, build, travel, draw, sew	
How much of a priority is money to me	High, medium, low	
If money were not an issue, what would I do with my life?		
What do I dislike? What do I not want to do?		
How big of a priority is fame?	High, medium, low	
What would I want people to say about me after I'm dead?	Generous, loving, hard working, friendly?	
Where to I envision myself in 25 years?		
Do I want to have a family and children someday?	Absolute must, yes but later, maybe	
What are my biggest defects? What could I improve?	Lazy, selfish, tardy, fearful, gluttonous, stubborn	
If I could change one thing about myself, what would it be?		
What are my biggest strengths? What do I want to keep doing?	Generous, loving, fun, strong, reliable, patient, adaptable	
Do I believe in God or some higher power? Describe that power.	Near, far, big, small, gentle, stern	
If I died today, what would I regret not doing?	Skydiving, getting married, traveling, working less	
Do people want to be around me? Do I want to be around people?		

CAREER CHOICES

Doctor	Janitor	Small business owner
Factory worker	Nurse	Professional athlete
Lawyer	Handyman	Restaurant operator
Engineer	Truck driver	Golf course operator
Bus driver	Salesman	Greens keeper
Hotel management	Waiter or waitress	Tennis professional
Fire fighter	Cook	Broadcaster
Police officer	Chef	Movie or television director
Parole officer	Construction management	Actor or actress
Teacher	Carpenter	Musician
Career counselor	Millwright	Dancer
Military professional	Electrician	Sculptor
Farmer	Pipe fitter	Model
Economist	Landscaper	Railroad worker
Artist	Pilot	Veterinarian
Writer	Auto mechanic	Circus clown
Journalist	Airline mechanic	Comedian
House painter	Public relations	Fitness instructor
Interior designer	Plumber	Cobbler
Tailor	Fashion designer	Banker
Stockbroker	Financial planner	Taxi driver
Brick layer	Steelworker	Bus driver
Travel agent	Animal trainer	Nanny
Roofer	Barber or hair stylist	Cashier
Receptionist	Administrative assistant	Judge
Politician	Public service	Non profit administrator
Importer/exporter	Banker	Clerk
Machine repairman	Fashion designer	Sportscaster

Patrick Shearer

JOB HUNT PREPARATIONS

✔ ☐	ACTION	NOTES
	EARLY QUESTIONS	
	What do I want to do?	
	What am I good at?	
	What skills can I leverage?	
	What do I absolutely not want to do?	
	Who would I want to work for?	
	Where do I want to live?	
	How much money do I want to earn?	
	What would I do if money were not a factor?	
	When would I want to make this career change?	
	GETTING READY	
	Build up money in savings	
	Consider hiring a placement service	
	Write resume	
	Practice for interviews	
	Research companies your interested in working for	
	Ask yourself why someone should hire you	
	Purchase interview attire	
	Write generic cover letter	
	Speak to someone in your desired field	
	Haircut and grooming	
	Develop a filing and tracking system	

TYPES OF HOBBIES

Stamp collecting	Restoring old automobiles	Scuba diving
Coin collecting	Carpentry/home improvement	Snorkeling
Trivia expert	Real estate	Boating
Golf	Traveling	Private pilot
Tennis	Collecting anything	Volunteer
Running	Become an expert at something	Teach part time
Skiing (snow or water)	History buff	Go to school
Reading	Painting	Wood carving
Working out	Dancing	Musical instrument
Model airplanes	Writing	Horse racing
Model trains	Walking	Actor/actress
Model cars	Swimming	Write/read poetry
Model boats	Attend sporting events	Arts and crafts

EXERCISE OPTIONS

Running	Tennis
Jogging	Bowling
Walking	Golf
Basketball	Bicycling
Hockey	Jumping rope
Softball	Treadmill
Martial arts	Lifting weights
Yoga	Stationary bicycle
Walking your dog	Handball
Downhill skiing	Racquetball
Cross country skiing	Squash
Water skiing	Coaching
Swimming	Paintball
Hiking	Laser tag
Mountain climbing	Rock climbing
Kayaking	Rowing
Canoeing	Yard work

PET CHOICES

Dog

Cat

Fish—freshwater or saltwater

Hamster

Gerbil

Snake

Lizard

Monkey

Horse or pony

Bird

Ferret

Ant Farm

Tarantula

Squirrel

Parrot

Turtle

Rabbit

AROUND THE HOUSE

PACKING FOR THE COTTAGE

CLOTHING

Swimming suits
Towels
Sweatshirt
Pants
Shorts
Undergarments
Pajamas
Socks
Shoes
Sandals
Belt
T-shirts

OTHER

Sunglasses
Life jackets
Book or magazine to read
DVD or video tapes
Music
Hat
Tobacco products
Lighter
Camera
Cell phone (maybe)
Baby supplies
Map
Games

FOOD

Coolers and ice
Meats (breakfast, lunch and dinner)
Vegetables
Fruits
Milk
Eggs
Bread
Cereals
Snacks
Dip
Desserts
Soda (diet and regular)
Water

TOILETRIES

Toothbrush
Toothpaste
Dental Floss
Soap
Comb and/or brush
Shampoo and conditioner
Deodorant
Hair ties
Lotion
Sunscreen or tanning oil
Razor
Shaving cream
Mouth wash

THINGS TO CONSIDER

Leave the blow dryer at home
Leave the cosmetics with the blow dryer
Leave the pager at home
Pack less food and shop at the local store
How long will we be gone—do I have enough of everything?
Do we need any dress clothes?
How much money will we need?

PACKING FOR A DAY AT THE BEACH

Sunglasses

Sunscreen or tanning oil

Chairs

Cooler

Ice

Beverages (for kids and adults)

Snacks

Towels

Umbrella

Change of clothes

Pail and shovel

Toys or games

Hat

Sandals

Money

Small table

Something to read

Radio, stereo or CD player

Binoculars

Wagon (to carry items from the car)

Sweatshirt for the evening

Watch with timer and alarm

Cups

Plates

Napkins

Eating utensils

Camera or camcorder

Pen or pencil

Tobacco products

Roller blades or skateboard

KITCHEN UTENSILS

Table knives	Blender
Forks	Mixer
Spoons	Toaster
Tongs	Toaster oven
Soup ladle	Radio and/or TV
Serving spoons	Crock pot
Serving forks	Dinner plates
Can opener	Salad plates
Measuring cups	Coffee mugs
Measuring spoons	Water glasses
Pots and pans	Juice glasses
Spatula	Bowls
Wooden spoon	Sugar bowl
Pasta strainer	Steak knives
Serving bowls	Cutlery
Meat thermometer	Bottle opener
Cutting board	Snack trays
Butter dish	Toothpicks
Nut cracker and picks	Plastic containers for leftovers
Measuring spoons	Egg whip

Patrick Shearer

GROCERY LIST

Canned Goods	Dry Goods	Fruit	Condiments
Diced Tomatoes	Cereal	Apples	Ketchup
Tomato Paste		Oranges	Mustard
Soup	Oatmeal	Grapefruit	Mayonnaise
Mushrooms	Saltines	Berries	Steak sauce
Spaghetti sauce	Crackers		BBQ sauce
Pineapple		Pears	Peanut butter
Mandarin oranges	Peanuts	Bananas	Jelly/Jam
Chili		Peaches	Salad dressing
Broth			Relish
Chocolate mix	**Frozen**	**Paper**	Pickles
	Chicken wings	Toilet paper	Syrup
Baking Products	Appetizers	Napkins	Salt
Olive oil	Vegetables	Paper towels	Pepper
Vegetable oil	Frozen dinners	Facial tissue	Hot sauce
Yeast	Orange Juice		
Gravy mix	Pizza	**Toiletries**	**Dairy**
Baking powder		Toothpaste	Milk
Baking soda		Soap	½ + ½
Flour	**Meat**	Shampoo	Eggs
Sugar	Lunchmeat	Razors	Butter
Brown Sugar	Hamburger	Floss	Yogurt
Corn Starch	Turkey	Shaving cream	Cheese
Powder sugar	Chicken	Deodorant	Cottage cheese
Spices	Steak	Feminine items	Sour cream
	Pork		Orange Juice
Cupcakes	Bacon		
Brownie mix	Sausage	Lotions	**Other**
B-day candles			Baby supplies
Cookie mix		Bandages	
Cake mix	**Vegetables**		Aluminum foil
Frosting	Lettuce	**Cleaners**	Plastic wrap
	Tomato	Laundry soap	Medicines
Beverages	Celery	Dish soap	
Soda-regular	Carrots	Bathroom	Batteries
Soda-diet	Green peppers	Kitchen	
Bottled water		Sponges	
Coffee-regular		Window	
Coffee-decaf		Bleach	

MONTHLY BUDGET

EXPENSE	BUDGETED EXPENSE	ACTUAL EXPENSE
Mortgage One		
Mortgage Two		
Taxes		
Home insurance		
Car payment		
Car payment		
Car insurance		
Car registration		
Car repair		
Gasoline		
Electrical utility		
Gas utility		
Cable or satellite TV		
Cell phone		
Home Phone		
Groceries		
Baby expenses		
Clothing and shoes		
Medical expenses		
Babysitting		
Haircuts and styling		
House cleaning		
Home improvement		
Dry cleaning		
Dining out		
Tuition and education		
Pocket money		
Charity		
Vacation		
Hobbies		
Health insurance		
Life insurance		
Gas		
Special events		
Entertainment		
Other:		
Other:		
Other:		
TOTAL EXPENSES		

TIPS FOR SAVING MONEY

#	Savings Idea	Notes/Expected Savings
1	Use direct deposit, never touch your paycheck	
2	Have savings deducted directly from you paycheck	
3	Don't get an ATM card	
4	Keep your credit card in a safe deposit box	
5	Take the soda bottles back	
6	Collect pocket change and deposit it every three months	
7	Take you lunch to work at least one day per week	
8	Make your own coffee before work	
9	One less can of soda or juice per day---drink tap water	
10	Get the least expensive cable television package	
11	Clip coupons from the newspaper	
12	Get the grocery store savings card	
13	Use the lowest octane gasoline (see the owner's manual)	
14	Buy groceries with cash only	
15	Buy in bulk	
16	Cancel one magazine or newspaper subscription	
17	Switch to one bargain brand or generic product	
18	Become a regular at the dollar store	
19	Split an entrée or dessert at dinner instead of buying two	
20	Avoid all late fees (mortgage, video, utility bills)	
21	Switch to no fee checking or savings accounts	

Patrick Shearer

BLANK CHECKLIST FOR _____ *

✔ ☐	ITEM	NOTES

* Use this table to build you own checklist

BLANK CHECKLIST FOR _____ *

✔ ☐	ITEM	NOTES

* Use this table to build you own checklist

NOTES

NOTES

NOTES

NOTES

NOTES

NOTES

NOTES

NOTES

NOTES

NOTES

NOTES

ABOUT THE AUTHOR

Pat Shearer is a husband, father and business professional. While clearing out some drawers at home he noticed that he and his wife had inadvertently pieced together a collection of lists that they had been using to handle things like picking baby names, packing for vacation, and buying a house. By coupling this real life experience with eight years in the Navy using checklists to handle every situation from cooking dinner to firing torpedoes, the author created *The Book of Checklists and Choices*. The book was expanded to include other checklists that would've come in handy as the author made his way through life. Although his two master's degrees look good on the wall it was the daily battles with gift decisions and party planning that provided the motivation for this book.

www.ingramcontent.com/pod-product-compliance
Lightning Source LLC
Chambersburg PA
CBHW080420290526
45791CB00008BA/2350